2018

MART CARDS: CHANGING THE FACE OF INFORMATION
IIS BY: Anthony Sorrell, BSBA MIS

004-2014 WHERE A.I. BEGAN

NTHONY SORRELL TECH

SMART CARDS: CHANGING THE FACE OF INFORMATION MIS 359

BY: Anthony Sorrell, BSBA MIS

SMART CARDS: CHANGING THE FACE OF INFORMATION MIS 359

BY: Anthony Sorrell, BSBA MIS 2004

What is a Smart Card?

A *'Smart Card'* simply put is a *computer* on a card. Most *smart cards* today are more powerful than the first PCs. Generally, a *smart card* is used when *memory* needs to be protected from general *access*. The *memory* is usually protected by means of a *code, password,* or other *authentication method* – much like an ATM code protects *access* to your bank account, except with *smart cards*; the code and *account information*; are all kept on *a single card* instead of the regional bank terminals used with Automatic Tellers. Basically, a *smart card* is a card with an embedded computer *chip*. The chip can either be a microprocessor with *internal memory*, or a memory chip with *non-programmable logic.* There are smart cards known as *'Contact'* or *'Integrated Circuit Cards'*; with a chip connection that requires a *direct physical contact* with an electromagnetic interface*'*; or *'Contactless'* cards, that require only *remote* or *wireless contact* with the interface.[i]

Smart Card Types

Contact smart cards are the size of a conventional credit or debit card with a *single embedded integrated circuit* chip that contains *just* memory or memory *plus* a microprocessor. A *contact smart card* requires insertion into a *smart card reader* with a direct connection to a conductive micro-module on the surface of the card (typically gold plated). It is through these physical contact points, that transmission of commands, data, and card status takes place. Chips that contain both memory and a microprocessor are similar to a small floppy disk, except they contain an "intelligent" controller used to securely add, delete, change, and update information contained in memory. The more sophisticated microprocessor chips have state-of-the-art security features built in to protect the contents of memory from unauthorized access. This type of e-card is used in a wide variety of applications including network security, vending - such as ticket purchase, college meal plans, electronic cash and e-commerce, government IDs, campus IDs, health cards, and several other applications.

How is a chip card different from the magnetic stripe cards? ….

What is a Smart Card?

A *'**Smart Card**'* simply put is a *computer* on a card. Most **smart cards** today are more powerful than the first PCs. Generally, a *smart card* is used when *memory* needs to be protected from general *access*. The *memory* is usually protected by means of a *code, password,* or other *authentication method* – much like an ATM code protects *access* to your bank account, except with *smart cards*; the code and *account information*; are all kept on *a single card* instead of the regional bank terminals used with Automatic Tellers. Basically, a *smart card* is a card with an embedded computer *chip*. The chip can either be a microprocessor with *internal memory*, or a memory chip with *non-programmable logic.*

There are smart cards known as *'**Contact**'* or *'**Integrated Circuit Cards**'*; with a chip connection that requires a *direct physical contact* with an electromagnetic interface'; or *'**Contactless**'* cards, that require only *remote* or *wireless contact* with the interface.[i]

Smart Card Types

Contact smart cards are the size of a conventional credit or debit card with a *single embedded integrated circuit* chip that contains *just* memory or memory *plus* a microprocessor.

A **contact** smart card requires insertion into a *smart card reader* with a direct connection to a conductive micro-module on the surface of the card (typically gold plated). It is through these physical contact points, that transmission of commands, data, and card status takes place. Chips that contain both memory and a microprocessor are similar to a small floppy disk, except they contain an "intelligent" controller used to securely add, delete, change, and update information contained in memory. The more sophisticated microprocessor chips have state-of-the-art security features built in to protect the contents of memory from unauthorized access. This type of e-card is used in a wide variety of applications including network security, vending - such as ticket purchase, college meal plans, electronic cash and e-commerce, government IDs, campus IDs, health cards, and several other applications.

With the **contactless** smart card, in addition to the features and functions found in contact smart cards, *contactless* smart cards contain an embedded antenna instead of contact pads attached to the chip for reading and writing information contained in the chip's memory. *Contactless* cards do not have to be inserted into a card acceptor device. Instead, they need only be passed within range of a radio frequency *acceptor* to read and store information in the chip. The typical range of operation is from about two and one half to four inches (2.5" to 4.0" US) (63.5mm to 99.06mm European) depending on the *acceptor* or *card interpreter (reader)* - range function.

Contactless smart cards are used in many of the same applications as *contact* smart cards, especially where the added convenience and speed of not having to insert the card into a reader is desirable. There is a growing acceptance of this type of card for both physical and logical access control applications. Student identification, electronic passport, vending, parking and tolls are common applications for *contactless* cards. Another type of *contactless* smart card is the *'**Proximity**'* **card**.

Proximity cards communicate through an antenna, like other *contactless* smart cards, except that they are read-only devices that generally have a greater range of operation. The range of peration for *proximity* smart cards is typically from two and one half to twenty inches (2.5" 20" US) (63.5mm to 508mm European) depending on the *card reader*. This distance is astly greater than its *contactless* predecessor; however, the *proximity* cards have limitations s well. It is possible to read a small amount of information with *proximity* cards such as an lentification code that is usually verified by a remote computer, however, it is not possible write information back to the card.

roximity cards or 'Prox' cards continue to grow in popularity because of the convenience ey offer in security, identification, and access control applications; used widely for such pplications as door access (i.e.-hotel, office, University, business, etc.) where fast, hands-ee operation is preferred.

Multi-Type Smart Cards

wo additional smart cards types derived from the *contact* and *contactless* cards that shall be uched on just briefly; are the ***'Combi'* card** and the ***'Hybrid'* card**. **Hybrid card** is the term iven to e-cards that contain two or more embedded chip technologies such as a *contactless* nart chip with its antenna, a *contact* smart chip with its contact pads, and/or a proximity nip with its antenna—all in a single card. The *contactless* chip is typically used for pplications demanding fast transaction times, like mass transit. The contact chip can be used applications requiring higher levels of security. The individual electronic components are ot connected to each other even though they share space in a single card. *Hybrid* cards offer unique solution for updating an existing ID-ing system.

his e-card allows you to accommodate the infrastructure and card technology of a legacy ystem while adding new applications and e-card technologies—all in a single ID card. The *ombi card*—also known as a ***'Dual-interface Card'***—has one (1) smart chip embedded in e card that can be *accessed* through either *contact pads* or an *embedded antenna*. This form f smart card is growing in popularity because it provides ease-of-use and high security in a ngle card product. Mass transit is expected to be one of the more popular applications for e combi card.[ii] [iii]

How is a chip card different from the magnetic stripe cards?

Existing magnetic stripe cards usually access an on-line data base. A chip card retains more aformation than can be accommodated on the typically used magnetic stripe card. A chip ard is like a 'Thinking Card'. It may make decision such as access to fund on a Bank pplication or date validity for parking, etc.; in most cases it has highly powerful nicroprocessor processing capabilities that allow it to do such task as manipulate information s well as data encryption and other secure actions. [iv]

Development

ISO-7816

SO is the "International Organization for Standardization." ISO-7816 1/2/3 define the Physical characteristics" (Part 1), "Dimensions and location of the contacts" (Part 2), and Electronic signals and transmission protocols" (Part 3) of virtually all Smart Cards in use today. These standards generally apply to all manufacturers of Smart Cards and Smart Card systems. There are a total of ten (10) parts to ISO standards for smart card Protocol and other smart card formats' Standards protocol.

The technology has its historical origin in the seventies when inventors in Germany, Japan, and France filed the original patents. Due to several factors, not least of which was the immaturity of the semiconductor technology, most work on smart cards was at the research and development level until the mid-eighties. Major rollouts such as the **'French National Visa Debit Card'** and **'France Telecom'** provided the industry with high volume test data and implementation opportunities. Since then, the computer chip-based industry, has been growing at tremendous rate is supplying more than a billion cards per year. The Smart Card is not a new technology, however. The Frenchmen, *Roland Moréno* - is widely accredited with inventing the first **smart card** prototype in 1974. However, it was the German, *Jurgen Dethloff* in Germany; and the Japanese, *Kunitaka Arimura* of the **'Arimura Technology Institute'** in Japan; who *filed* the *first patents* before *Moréno*. *Moréno's* worldwide *patents* covered the *'concept of embedding a microcontroller'* into a regular bank style plastic card. It was not surprising then that other visionaries within the card development industry viewed *Moréno's* concepts with enthusiasm.[v]

Data Transmissions of Smart Card

All communications to and from the smartcard are carried out over the C7 contact. Thus, only one party can communicate at a time, whether it is the card or the terminal. This is termed "half-duplex". Communication is always initiated by the terminal, which implies a type of client/server relationship between card and terminal.

After a card is inserted into a terminal, it is powered up by the terminal, executes a power-on-reset, and sends an Answer to Reset (ATR) to the terminal. The ATR is parsed, various parameters are extracted, and the terminal then submits the initial instruction to the card. The card generates a reply and sends it back to the terminal. The client/server relationship continues in this manner until processing is completed and the card is removed from the terminal.

The physical transmission layer is defined in ISO/IEC 7816-3. It defines the voltage level specifics which end up translating into the "0" and "1" bits.

Logically, there are several different protocols for exchanging information in the client/server relationship. They are designated "T=" plus a number

The two protocols most commonly seen are T=0 and T=1, T=0 being the most popular. A brief overview of the T=0 protocol is given below.

The references contain more detailed information and descriptions of all the protocols.

Figure: Typical: T=0{instruction}

[vi]

In the T=0 protocol, the terminal initiates communications by sending a 5 byte instruction header which includes a class byte (CLA), an instruction byte (INS), and three parameter bytes (P1, P2, and P3). This is followed optionally by a data section. Most commands are either incoming or outgoing from the card's perspective and the P3 byte specifies the length of the data that will be incoming or outgoing. Error checking is handled exclusively by a parity bit appended to each transmitted byte. If the card correctly receives the 5 bytes, it will return a one-byte acknowledgment equivalent to the received INS byte.

If the terminal is sending more data (incoming command) it will send the number of bytes it specified in P3. Now the card has received the complete instruction and can process it and generate a response. All commands have a two-byte response code, SW1 and SW2, which reports success or an error condition. If a successful command must return additional bytes,

The terminal and card communicate in this manner, using incoming or outgoing commands, until processing is complete.

Real World Smart Card Applications

Imagine leaving for work in the morning, walking out of your house and down the street to the subway station. As you enter the station, you walk right past the line at the ticket counter and through the turnstile, which automatically deducts the fare from a smart card in your hip pocket. Twenty minutes later, you get off the subway and grab a cup of coffee, paying with the same smart card. Arriving at work, you whip the card out again for the lobby security guard, who glances at the photo and waves you through. Now at your office door, you use the smart card/ID badge as a key, waving it past an RF reader on the wall.

Finally, as you sit down at your desk and boot up your PC, you slide the card—the same card—into a reader, enter your PIN and log on to the network. This scenario is the dream of every smart card manufacturer, issuer and integrator in the world. Put a smart card in everyone's hands and build the infrastructure so it can be used everywhere, for everything. Not just electronic purse and access control, but driver's licenses, national ID and health insurance cards, telecommunications, mobile commerce and more.

Privacy concerns aside—and there are plenty of them—rapid technological innovation and explosive adoption rates make this far-fetched scenario, well, not so far-fetched after all. While smart cards are years away from achieving critical mass in the United States for any of these uses, predictions of "hockey stick growth" in some segments are finally coming true. Last year, more than 41 million cards were manufactured for use in the U.S., a 45 percent increase over 2000, according to a Smart Card Alliance study released last month.

Year-to-year growth in shipments to the federal government topped 1,000 percent, while shipments to retail and financial institutions grew by 377 percent and 146 percent, respectively. Despite 2001's impressive growth, the U.S. remains at least a generation behind Asia and Europe in the use of smart cards. Smart cards are a part of the European culture and business system; in the U.S., it's going to require a whole shift in dynamics.

Smart cards have always been cool, but not always practical. Although their core functionality has remained unchanged for 30 years (see "What Is a Smart Card?" p. 34), recent developments have increased their practical viability. Memory. The single biggest driver of smart card growth, experts say, is their multi-applications capabilities. Today, most smart card manufacturers, are mass-producing 32K cards, which allow the same card to be used for multiple applications. For high-capacity applications, more expensive 64K and even 128K cards can be used.

The Washington Metropolitan Area Transit Authority (WMATA) has issued more than 210,000 smart cards to Metro subway and commuter train riders in the Washington, D.C., and Northern Virginia area. Riders can store up to $200 on a contactless smart card called SmarTrip. Small purchases (say, for example, paying at the gate when leaving a parking lot) using their smart credit card, rather than having to look for change. They can also be used for cross-channel marketing: via TV set-top boxes, the internet, and mobile phones.

The major credit card issuers are moving towards chip cards. American Express says it has issued 2.2 million of its chip-bearing Blue Cards in just 14 months. Visa expects its banks to issue seven million smart cards in the US over the next year. Visa is certainly covering its options. Along with STMicroelectronics, the company is launching a new smart card that will cost less than US$1. The new card is expected to accelerate the migration to chip and encourage others in the payment services marketplace to follow suit. Being developed in partnership with IBM; the card will provide a significant boost to banks looking for a cost effective way to introduce single application smart cards and to reduce fraud.

A smart card solution provider, and Target Corporation, the fourth largest general merchandise retailer in the United States have signed up to provide smart cards and in-home readers for the Target smart cards – Target smart card Visa format. Also, Target will be issuing smart cards through its Retailers National Bank affiliate and installing point of sale terminals that accept chip payment in all Target Stores in by autumn 2002, according to March 2002 report.

The Open Card Framework provides programmers with an interface for the development of smart card applications in Java. Implementations of Open Card can be 100% pure Java, or they can use existing card terminal implementations (a.k.a. *smart-card readers*) such as PC/SC. Open Card differs from PC/SC in that it promises to provide a uniform application interface for building smart card applications on the emerging new platforms, such as network computers, phones, automatic teller machines, and cable TV boxes.

Open Card can provide 100% pure Java smart card applications. Smart card applications often are not pure because they communicate with an external device or use libraries on the client. In order to use a smart card, you need to be able to read the card and communicate with it using an application. Open Card provides a framework for this by defining interfaces that must be implemented. The Open Card framework defines several of these interfaces. The card agent can then communicate with applications on the smart card via the card terminal in the context of a session.

There are over 300,000,000 GSM mobile telephones with smart cards which contain the mobile phone security and subscription information. The handset is personalized to the individual by inserting the card which contains its phone number on the network, billing information, and frequently call numbers. Almost every small dish TV satellite receiver uses a smart card as its removable security element and subscription information. There are over 4 million in the US alone between DirecTV, USSB and Echo Star. There are millions more in Europe and Asia.

Various countries with national health care programs have deployed smart card systems. The largest is the German solution which deployed over 80,000,000 cards in Germany and

Austria. There are over 100 countries worldwide that have reduced or eliminated coins from the pay phone system by issuing smart cards.[vii]

Smart Card Applications at Work

UNIVERSITY SMART ID

The **Universicard** is a management tool, designed to alleviate the monotonous and time-consuming administrative tasks of running a university. **Universicard** replaces numerous other systems used on campus and can ensure a smooth running management system. In addition, it is a unique advantage of being impossible to tamper with or be copied. Information about the

Universicard:

The life span of a Smartcard is minimum of 3 years. The microchip can perform more than 10,000 operations. There are three types of information inscribed on the card.

1. Permanent information (inscribed on the front of the card): Designated university code; Student number; Last name; First name; Date and Place of birth
2. Other information (inscribed on the back of the card): Nationality; Social security number; Health insurance policy number
3. Photograph of card holder

The following information is programmed into the Universicard microchip:

1. Permanent information (see above) this information cannot be modified once programmed.
2. Other information this information can be modified once programmed.
3. Micro processing facility which calculates a card holder's debit account
4. Validity dates of the card the expiration date can be updated upon re-enrolment.
5. Serial number of the card
6. Lost card code this code is used to temporarily invalidate the card if it is lost.

In Addition:

*The **Universicard** can be personalized for each university by adding school colours, logos, or mascots.*

Student access and frequency management:

Universicard can grant access to certain areas and to certain information on campus:

1) Direct access: University library; Parking lots; Specialized rooms (science labs, Computer labs, etc.); Certain Materials (videos, audio equipment, etc.); University buildings; Student housing

2) Indirect access: Access to interactive terminals on campus; the use of the card and the interactive terminals allows a dialogue between the professors and the students on subjects such as:

1. Information on the dates and location of exams
2. Results of exams and course work
3. Information concerning the lectures.

The use of plastic money:

The **Universicard** can manage different services using electronic plastic money. a) Payment for all: university services on campus; University-owned photocopiers, laser printers, fax machines, etc.; Books and materials; University restaurants, cafeteria, snack bar; Campus shops

The **Universicard** can also assure the automatic payment for services offered by non-university vendors on campus. b) Payment for all private franchise services on campus: Drink and food dispensers; Video games; Restaurants and bars[viii]

MASS TRANSIT

The first electronic fare collection modes were introduced in the United States in the 1970s on rail systems in Washington, D.C., and San Francisco. As electronic fare media developed for rail, so did the developments in bus technology, until eventually electronic fare collection began to set the standard in the industry.

From magnetic stripe cards to contactless smart cards, electronic media offer a host of options for transit agencies to customize their systems to accommodate just about every rider. Using automated fare collection systems gives the agency the choice of which type of non-cash payment method to use, and the options are extensive. "We are looking at adaptive technology to our fare boxes," says Todd Cull, general manager of Diamond Manufacturing in Kansas City, Mo. "There are technologies in the marketplace that can be used in conjunction with a mechanical box."

Depending on a number of variables, including the size of the transit area, the number of riders and the level of sophistication sought by the transit agency, several different electronic fare media options are available. A rapidly growing number of transit agencies are looking for a system that does more than just collect money. Manufacturers are developing and enhancing systems to be compatible with the emerging smart card technology. "Smart card systems are the next phase in fare collection evolution," says Kim Green, vice president at GFI Genfare, according to report.

"We are maximizing the useful management information that is available from our passenger and revenue collection data systems," Green says. Dallas Area Rapid Transit (DART), which is in the process of procuring a smart card system, heralds the data collection capabilities as one of the biggest advantages of smart card technology. "Theoretically, we can find out where along a bus route a person is boarding the bus, where they're getting off the bus and if they're transferring to another vehicle," says Matt Raymond, assistant vice president of advertising and marketing at DART. "We collect so much customer data that we'd be able to analyze that and provide better service." Manufacturers are now developing systems that make smart cards seamless between different types of transit and other applications, such as concessionary stores in stations. Because of the memory capacity and stored value capabilities of smart cards, their potential for use outside of fare collection knows no bounds.

WMATA and the Baltimore MTA are currently using the smart card capabilities to offer regional riders access to transit in Washington, D.C., Maryland and northern Virginia. The WMATA/MTA system allows different agencies to maintain their individual fare regulations. "The systems are adaptable and programmable so that everyone can maintain their own tariffs," says Greg Garback, executive officer for the department of finance and program development at WMATA. WMATA/MTA employs a clearinghouse to issue, maintain and service the smart card operation, according to the report. TransLink®, the regional project in San Francisco, is implementing a similar system to connect service between as many as 22 different agencies. Users will buy a contactless fare card that is valid at all agencies participating in the TransLink program. TransLink®, the regional project in San Francisco, is implementing a similar system to connect service between as many as 22 different agencies. Users will buy a contactless fare card that is valid at all agencies participating in the TransLink program.[ix]

THE FUTURE OF SMART CARDS/ WALLET-PHONES

The wallet phone is the next stage in the evolution of mobile phones. Wallet phones will soon become an essential part of the everyday life infrastructure. Wallet phones are pioneered by NTT-DoCoMo by combining a multi-application smart card with I-Mode phones. Wallet phones can be used as prepaid electronic cash, tickets, access control cards, authorizations to access corporate networks, membership cards for clubs and loyalty programs. Selected information, for example the remaining electronic cash balance, or some transaction records, can be directly read offline by the cell phone.

Wallet phones can contain all credit cards, entrance tickets, train tickets, air tickets, employee ID cards, and most other instruments we currently carry in our purse. Integration of multi-application smartcards into mobile phones, will make cell phones an essential part of our daily life infrastructure.

Cell phones in Japan will work as concert tickets, identification cards and electronic wallets in a new service by the nation's top mobile carrier, NTT DoCoMo, that uses smart card technology developed by Sony Corp. The service starts on a trial basis Wednesday and is the first result of NTT DoCoMo's partnership with Japanese electronics giant Sony that was announced in October, the mobile phone giant said. With a technology-savvy public eager for innovations, Japan leads the world in new cell phone features such as digital cameras and Internet links. People in some European countries and Taiwan can also use their mobile phones to access the Internet. In South Korea, cell phones use infrared and radio waves to make electronic payments.

Developed by Sony, the technology dubbed FeliCa uses a computer chip embedded in a card that permits payments for purchases or train tickets. Users just need to hold the cards near special machines which communicate with the chips. Some 19 million FeliCa cards are now being used in Japan for train passes or electronic payments, according to Sony. The new service, which uses that technology in cell phones, was demonstrated by the various providers to the media on Monday. In one service, users download a concert or movie ticket from an Internet site, paying with a credit card. The user then brings the mobile phone to the theater for quick prepaid entry. Tokyo computer-game maker Sega Corp. will also participate in the new service by allowing people to pay in advance for arcade games by putting cash into a special machine that relays that information into a FeliCa-equipped cell phone, Sega officials said. Japanese airline All Nippon Airways said it will offer an advance check-in service by mobile phone. The user brings the FeliCa cell phone to the airport counter, after registering by mobile Internet. Information such as names and seat numbers shows up on an airport monitor, though passports and plane tickets are still needed. The demonstrations showed that the FeliCa cell phone can be handy for other uses such as employee identification and shopping discount points. During the trial service, which continues until the summer of next year, NTT DoCoMo will supply 27 service providers with two handset models. A commercial service is being planned for sometime next year, but details are still undecided. Sony's FeliCa smart card technology, developed in 1988, is widely used in Japanese train systems and is also used in Hong Kong. NTT DoCoMo has said it hopes to offer the FeliCa service overseas.[x]

SECURITY ISSUE: A CASE STUDY – SATTELLITE TELEVISION

DirecTV AccessCard (ISO7816 SmartCard)

There are at least *4 generations* of Smart Cards issued by **DirecTV.**
The security codes for the first 3 generations of cards have been broken and are being replaced by *DirecTV* with P4's (DirecTV fourth Generation Smart Cards). There is also a rumoured 5th Generation Card, said to be completely developed "in-house" at *DirecTV*. The first 4 generations were developed in full or part by **NDS (Smart card provider)** and are based off the **NDS** *VideoGuard system.*

The current and previous *DirecTV Access Cards*, designed and made by **NDS**, are compatible with ISO 7816 format devices. It is *DirecTV's* position that Smart Card Readers/Writers, **Universal Smart Card Terminal's (USCT's) or Smart Card Repair Terminals**, and Emulators (An "emulator" is a device that acts like or takes the place of another device, usually a CPU or Microprocessor [note: a Smart Card is nearly identical to a microprocessor.]); are "pirate access devices" and "designed primarily" for receiving *DirecTV* service for free.

Additionally, they claim USCTs were designed specifically for *DirecTV Access Cards*; despite the fact that *DirecTV* Smart Cards were purposely designed by **NDS** to comply with the previously-defined ISO 7816 specifications that USCTs have always used; and **NDS** "out-sourced" some or all of the Smart Card technology it used for the *DirecTV* Access Cards from other companies that already make ISO 7816 Smart Cards. Thus, it is no surprise that USCTs that are compatible with ISO 7816 standards also work on *DirecTV Access Cards*.(Legal Case Study: DirecTV Security In **APPENDIX B**)[xi]

Conclusion

Because **smart cards** are indeed mini-computers; it's difficult to predict the variety of applications that will be possible with them in the future. It's quite possible that **smart cards** will follow the same trend of rapid increases in processing power within the computer industry has experienced, following *"Moore's Law"*; and doubling in performance while cost divide every eighteen months. **Smart cards** have proven to be quite useful as a *transaction/authorization/identification* medium in European and Asian countries. As their capabilities grow, they could become the ultimate thin client; eventually replacing all of the things we carry around in our wallets: including credit cards, licenses, cash; and even including family photographs. By containing various identification certificates, **smart cards** could be used to uniquely identify attributes of ourselves no matter where we are or to which *computer network* we are attached.

As a *technology-oriented society*; as we focus on the nature of the *state-of-the-art* of **smart cards** technology and their use in computer and network *security systems; applications and integrations*; hopefully we may look to the future. This is the goal that will bring this nation closer the information revolution.

APPENDIX A

⇓SMART CARD

CONTACTLESS SMART CARD ◊

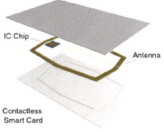

IC Chip

Antenna

Contactless
Smart Card

⇓HYBRID SMART CARD

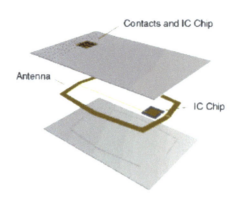

COMBI SMART CARD◊

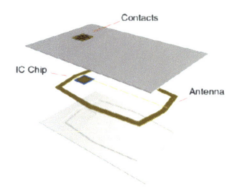

PROXIMITY SMART CARD◊

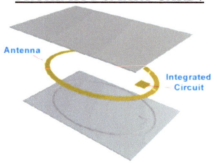

Courtesy of Fargo.com

APPENDIX B

DirecTV's letters and lawsuits accuse people of purchasing and using "illegal signal theft equipment" and "pirate access devices." But what exactly are these "accused" devices and how do they work? Current smart card technology, including many of the legitimate uses that these devices have uses that should not be collateral damage in DirecTV's fight against satellite signal piracy.

Why is DirecTV threatening innocent people?

In the past year or so, satellite TV giant DirecTV has sent ominous letters to an estimated 100,000 individuals, accusing them of purchasing *"illegal signal theft equipment"* and *"pirate access devices"* and threatening to haul them into court for stealing DirecTV. The letter tells the unlucky recipients that the prospect of a pricey legal battle will go away if they pay up, to the tune of $3,500 in most cases. Yet, in too many cases, the recipients of the letters have never intercepted DirecTV's signal. They merely possess smart card technology. Without proof of a violation of law, DirecTV's unsubstantiated threats to sue are an abuse of the legal system.

DirecTV's campaign began with a series of raids on Internet Web sites. Armed with Digital Millennium Copyright Act, DirecTV paid visits to well-known online vendors like Whiteviper, took over their *Web sites*, and went home with their customer records.

Next, groups of DirecTV enforcers with euphemistic names such as the "End User Development Group" started sending threat letters and staffing the call center. The word to worried technology researchers and customers: Pay now, or pay a lot more later in court—possibly up to $100,000.

Most recently, DirecTV has been making good on its threats to sue, even against people who expressly explained to DirecTV the legitimate uses they were pursuing such as scientific research or home-brewed security systems. Undeterred, the company has brought *nearly 9,000 lawsuits* in federal district courts across the country.

In its letters, DirecTV often makes an unjustified and dangerous legal leap: that purchasing technology with a possible illegal use (intercepting DirecTV's signal) is illegal, even if you haven't been breaking the law by actually intercepting the signal. This "guilty until proven innocent" campaign has presented a tough call for all the non-pirates targeted by DirecTV: Pay thousands of dollars to stop DirecTV's threats or face a long and expensive legal battle to prove you are innocent.
When innocent people end up paying corporate behemoths for crimes they didn' commit, something is wrong.

Who's winning?

By most reports, DirecTV has talked plenty of people into settling, including some who never stole a second of signal. But so far, this Goliath hasn't had a single meaningful win against an innocent end user in court. It may be wise for people who've been breaking the law by stealing DTV to settle out of court. But for the innocent purchasers, DirecTV doesn't have proof that they've ever intercepted a single DirecTV program, and therefore shouldn't be able to win a legal case.

The law prohibits stealing signals, not purchasing smart card readers, and to prevail, DirecTV must have evidence of actual interception. (Get the full legal analysis **here**.) But there's no evidence against thousands of innocent users targeted by DirecTV. In many cases, DirecTV is simply assuming that piracy is happening without a single shred of proof.

In the first substantive court decisions, just rolling in now, lack of proof has spelled losses for DirecTV. ***A Michigan judge ruled*** that a purchase invoice didn't look like proof to him when the defendant didn't even own a DirecTV dish. (The judge granted a motion for reconsideration when DirecTV produced evidence that the defendant had purchased DirecTV equipment in the past.) In Florida, ***a court recently threw out*** DirecTV's long-shot attempt to make mere possession of a device illegal. And an Ohio judge ***dismissed a slew of cases*** in which DirecTV lumped together 320 unrelated defendants in 44 complaints, scolding the deep-pocketed corporation for trying to defraud the public of proper filing fees.

However, efforts to take DirecTV to task for threatening innocent people and filing frivolous lawsuits have so far failed. A ***California class action lawsuit*** against DirecTV for extortion lost in the first round (it's now on appeal). Defendants have had ***little luck with counterclaims*** even when they win a dismissal. And though the law would allow DirecTV to recover its ***attorney fees*** if it ever won a case, defendants don't recoup the money they spend on lawyers and court costs no matter how innocent they are.

What is a Smart Card?

ANTHONY SORRELL - BSBA MIS

SMART CARDS: CHANGING THE FACE
OF INFORMATION MIS 359

References:

"Is the US Ready For Smart Cards Yet?" *By Robin Clark*
www.wisemarket.com

"A Smart Card for Everyone?" *By Andy Britney*
March 2002; www.forbes.com

"Some Aspects of the History of Smart Cards" *By Peter Hawkins and BTG Limited;*
International Smartcard Industry Guide

"Wallet Phones-Internet Phone with Smartcards"; "Wallet Phone Report"
www.eurotechnology.com

"Smart Card Primer"; ISO Standards: *BY Charles Cagliostro; Smartcard Alliance*

Smartcard Applications *HealthData Products*
www.hdata.com

Smartcard Group: *www.smartcard.co/uk*

www.silo.silicon.vally.com
www.usa.visa.com
www.direcTVdefence.org
www.techmarket.com
www.sspsouvtrans.com
www.fargo.com

---

[i] Excerpt References From: *The SmartCard Alliance: Smart Card Technology* ;
www.silo.silicon.vally.com
[ii] Excerpt References From: *Fargo Electronics: Smart card Technology-Smart card*
types
[iii] Illustrations of Varied Smart card Types Within **APPENDIX B**: *Courtesy of -Fargo Electronics*
[iv] References From: *HealthData products and services:* webmaster@hdata.com
[v] References From: *The SmartCard Alliance: Smart Card Standards; Smart Card*
Group: History of Smart cards;" Some Aspects of The History of Smart Cards":
International Smartcard Industry Guide
[vi] Diagram and Excerpt References From: *www.sspsouvtrans.com*
[vii] Excerpts From:" *Is the US Ready for Smart Cards Yet?" www.*
thewisemarket.com; "A Smart Card For Everyone?" www.Forbes.com
[viii] Application References From: *HealthData products and services:*
webmaster@hdata.com
[ix] "Smart Card Technology Just Got Smarter" MASS Transit Applications:
[x] Excerpt References From:" *Wallet phones - internet phones with smartcards":*
www.eurotechnology.com; "Wallet Phone Report": www.eurotechnology.com
[xi] Report based on DirecTV Legal Security Law Suits-In **APPENDIX B**

www.ingramcontent.com/pod-product-compliance
Lightning Source LLC
Chambersburg PA
CBHW041148050326
40689CB00001B/537

* 9 7 8 1 5 4 9 8 6 4 5 8 2 *